The Emotionalists

MW01516428

Writer, director, and dr̶.̶.̶.̶ ̶.̶.̶.̶.̶.̶.̶.̶.̶.̶.̶.̶.̶.̶.̶.̶.̶.̶.̶ ̶.̶.̶.̶ Sky Gilbert was artistic director of Buddies in Bad Times Theatre (Toronto) for eighteen years. He left in 1997 to pursue writing. Two novels, *Guilty* (1998) and *St. Stephens* (Insomnia Press 1999), as well as a memoir of Buddies, *Ejaculations from the Charm Factory* (ECW 2000), soon followed. Blizzard Publishing published his Buddies hit *Play Murder* in 1995.

theEmotionalists

by
Sky Gilbert

BLIZZARD PUBLISHING
Winnipeg • Niagara Falls

First published 2000 in Canada and 2001 in the United States by
Blizzard Publishing Inc.
73 Furby Street, Winnipeg, Canada R3C 2A2.

Distributed in the United States by General Distribution Services,
4500 Witmer Industrial Estates, Niagara Falls, NY 14305–1386.

Cover art by Timothy Philippi.
Cover design by Otium.
Printed for Blizzard Publishing in Canada.

5   4   3   2   1

Blizzard Publishing gratefully acknowledges the support of the
Manitoba Arts Council, the Canada Council for the Arts, and the
Government of Canada through the Book Publishing Industry
Development Program for our publishing program.

Cataloguing in Publication Data

Gilbert, Sky.
   The emotionalists.
   ISBN 0-55331-001-2
1. Rand, Ayn—Drama.   I. Title.

PS8563.I4743 E48 2000   C812'.54   C00–920193–9
PR9199.3.G5248 E48 2000

to my own
"Ayneleh" (Bright Eyes) Ian

"Emotions are not tools of cognition."
—Ayn Rand

"Life imitates Art far more than Art imitates Life."
—Oscar Wilde

The Emotionalists was first produced by the Cabaret Company at The Music Gallery, Toronto, from March 23 to April 7, 2000, with the following cast:

AYN RAND	Ellen-Ray Hennessy
FRANK O'CONNOR	Philip Shepherd
NATHANIEL BRANDEN	Alex Poch-Goldin
BARBARA BRANDEN	Veronika Hurnik
MARCEL PIN	Gil Garratt
BRUCE LEVER	Patrick Connor

Directed by Sky Gilbert
Sets and lights by Steve Lucas
Costumes by Wendy White
Stage Manager: Sallie Klein

Introduction

Ayn Rand was my mentor.

These days, when anybody asks me about my literary "influences" I usually cite Joe Orton, Dennis Cooper, and James Purdy. But that's not completely honest. Those are certainly my most recent literary influences. But for most of my teen years, I was caught up in the heady thrall of Ayn Rand.

For those of you who don't know Ayn Rand's work, she wrote three novels: *We the Living*, *The Fountainhead*, and *Atlas Shrugged*, which were published in the U.S. between 1936 and 1957. Though ravaged by most serious literary critics, they were enormously popular with the public. (*The Fountainhead* is often listed right under the Bible on all-time bestseller lists.) Rand's ideas spawned a philosophical movement in the late sixties, led by Ayn Rand and her protégé Nathaniel Branden. Their philosophy was called "Objectivism."

If you've read something by or about Ayn Rand, you probably either love her or hate her. Like Liza Minelli, Bette Midler, and Barbra Streisand, she's a loud American. And like those entertainers, she's (as I like to say) all flash and no pan.

You see, when it comes to Ayn Rand, I'm a fan of her fiction but a bitter enemy of her ideas. Why? I think the novels are fabulous trash. Her cardboard romantic characters and creaky melodramtic plots are made compelling by the passion of her writing. If one approaches the novels with a young and open heart, one cannot help but be enraptured. Her ideas, on the other hand, are not just repellent, but dangerous. I don't say this just because Rand is an unashamed champion of capitalism, egotism, and selfishness. I say this because her novels changed the life of one lonely, unhappy teenager (myself), and certainly not for the better.

I read *The Fountainhead*, as most people do, when I was very young (thirteen years old). Rand's vision of a perfect egotist, a lone creative artist/intellectual, was embodied in her hero Howard Roark (and played by Gary Cooper in the stunningly awful Hollywood film of the book). Well, at age thirteen, I believed I *was* Howard Roark.

It made sense at the time. After all, I didn't fit in with my classmates. All they wanted to do was gossip about parties, sports, and rock and roll. Being a closeted effeminate homo, parties and sports were the last thing that interested me. Of course I was unwilling to admit to myself, or to anyone else, that I was gay, so I eagerly embraced Ayn Rand's theories. They were a comfortable rationale for my position as social outcast. Clearly I was a genius—superior to my mediocre peers. I imagined that I would one day become an architect. I never missed a CNE home show, rushing home to scribble fanciful floorplans in my school notebooks. I walked alone on windy rainy afternoons near statuesque structures (a particular favorite were the IBM buildings dotting a hill at Eglinton and Don Mills Road), and pondered my heroic status as a misunderstood prodigy. I wrote a novel. My hero was an iconoclastic romantic composer who created music which was one step beyond atonal. I subscribed to *The Objectivist Newsletter*—a monthly magazine published by Ayn Rand and Nathaniel Branden. I wore a gold-plated bracelet on my wrist for all to see, proudly emblazoned with a dollar sign (Rand's favorite symbol).

Yes, I was a teenage nut. Harmless youthful idealism, you might say? Unfortunately not. Far more destructive than Rand's advocacy for the free market (ideas which have had huge influence; one of her disciples—Alan Greenspan—is commander-in-chief of the U.S. economy today) are her psychologyical theories, which were promoted by Nathaniel Branden. Branden, an ambitious man many years her junior, became her lover. And this was with the full permission of Branden's wife and Rand's husband. Ironically (in light of their personal life) Rand and Branden's theories championed the supremacy of reason over emotion. That thoughts, in effect, can rule the heart.

As a young, self-hating gay man, I welcomed Rand's puritanism. I imagined I could argue myself out of homosexuality. I laboured over endless journal passages, arguing the advantages and disadvantages of being gay, always reminding myself that gay was "irrational."

It didn't work. Finally, at age twenty-nine, after many failed and frustrating heterosexual relationships, I dumped Ayn Rand in the garbage and came out of the closet.

Recently, I discovered I was not the only one wrestling with the effects of her ideas. Others have found that taking Rand's enthralling novels too seriously can have an adverse effect, as Jeff Walker's recent *The Ayn Rand Cult* (Open Court, 1999) proves. This thought-provoking analysis of the damage wrought by Rand's philosophy made me realize that my obsession with her had almost ruined my life.

On the other hand, I wouldn't want to stop adolescents from reading Ayn Rand, any more then I'd try and stop kids from reading C. S. Lewis's Narnia books (which are, after all, just thinly-disguised Christian propaganda).

Literature is dangerous. But so is life.

And that, really, is what it's all about.

—Sky Gilbert,
October 2000

A Note on the Set

All the locales of the play should be located on one set, so that there are no set changes during the acts. The main part of the stage should be taken up with Rand's living-room. In Act One, a very small area can be reserved for the flower shop. In Act Two a bench in front of the Brandens' Doorway can replace this flower shop. The cliff, in the original production, was set on top of the hallway, as an area only lit during Act Two.

As for the hallways, there are two. The first, *apartment* hallway is inside Rand's apartment connecting the living-room to the front door. It would be better if the characters were not visible when they were in this hallway. The second *building* hallway is outside the apartment, and can simply be a small area in front of the door to the apartment (still indoors). So when Barbara and Nathaniel come to visit, their argument takes place in the *building* hallway, and then they are let into the *apartment* hallway (which is connected to the rest of the house) before meeting Ayn in the living-room.

Characters

AYN RAND: A philosopher; fifty years old
FRANK O'CONNOR: her husband, same age
NATHANIEL BRANDEN: a therapist, twenty-five years old
BARBARA BRANDEN: his wife, same age
MARCEL PIN: a florist; twenty-five years old
BRUCE LEVER: A gay man; thirty-five years old

Setting

New York City, 1955.

*This play is a work of fiction, not history.
Although inspired by historical events, it is
not intended to be read as fact.*

Act One

(Lights up on a chair in a darkened room. A woman, dimly viewed, is sitting, holding a telephone receiver, listening. She lights a cigarette. Then she begins talking with a thick Russian accent. The image is very romantic.)

AYN: Should we call it that? Are those the words you should use to warn her? *(She laughs helplessly.)* Of course the words are important. Don't make me laugh now. You mustn't make me laugh. We have to be serious. Oh ... we must be so serious. *(She laughs again. Then she turns quickly, thinking she's heard something.)* Shhh! I thought I heard—*(But there is no noise.)* no it's all right. Yes, only a few more minutes my darling one and then—yes you are my darling one, you are the only one, the one and only. You know, I must tell you that for me these months have been like living in Russia. *(Pause.)* Yes, in Russia, because in that horrible place there was no joy whatsoever, except perhaps in the few chords of music, the lighthearted operettas of Kalman and Lehar. And I imagined a world, another world where beauty might dare to exist—where princes danced and laughed. But I had to keep that world a secret; I had to keep my joy a secret—why? Because first of all we weren't to listen to such music, it was not a music of the people, a music of altruism and then—Shhhh!

(She hides the phone and freezes. We hear a knock at the door and see MARCEL poised outside. She whispers urgently.)

Today, yes today, it must be today. Goodbye.

(She hangs up the phone and smokes. The footsteps get louder. Then the door opens. We see FRANK's ominous and dramatic silhouette illuminated by the light coming from the a tiny hallway stage right.)

FRANK: Ayn?

AYN: Yes.

FRANK: What are you doing? Why are you sitting here in the dark?

AYN: I was—Frank I was ... I was thinking.

FRANK: I see. You usually do your thinking with the lights on.

AYN: Yes but ... this was a very difficult chapter.

FRANK: Oh. Ayn I came to tell you—

> *(He strides boldly into the room and then flicks on the light and opens the curtains. She shields her eyes. We are suddenly in a very bright room. There is a piano in the corner. One is struck by the room's modern sunlit quality; very California for a New York apartment circa 1955—very Frank Lloyd Wright. After the darkness the light is almost blinding.)*

AYN: Yes.

FRANK: There's someone here to see you.

AYN: Now?

FRANK: Yes.

AYN: I'm not expecting anyone. Except of course Nathaniel and Barbara.

FRANK: He's very persistent.

AYN: But now is the worst time.

FRANK: The worst? Why?

AYN: *(Very testily.)* What I mean is, it's not a good time.

FRANK: *(Indulgently.)* He *claims* to be an Objectivist.

AYN: He does?

FRANK: Yes.

AYN: Well I should see him then.

FRANK: He's waiting in the hallway.

AYN: Thank you. *(Pause.)* Darling.

FRANK: You're welcome.

> *(Pause. They stare at each other.)*

Dearest.

> *(An awkward moment.)*

AYN: I should see him now?

FRANK: Yes.

AYN: *(Testily.)* Well then can you get him?

> *(FRANK opens the front door to a tiny hallway and MARCEL enters—his hat in his hands. The room makes him look very small and uncomfortable. He wears a somewhat shabby suit. Unlike FRANK, who is wearing a breezy casual period shirt, he doesn't blend in with the surroundings.)*

FRANK: Ayn, this is Mr. Pin.

AYN: Mr. Pin.

MARCEL: Miss Rand?

AYN: Yes.

MARCEL: What an enormous pleasure I … almost don't know what to say.

AYN: Why not sit down.

MARCEL: Yes, thank you, of course.

> *(MARCEL sits. FRANK slides easily out of the room; as is his usual practice.)*

Is he your ummm … husband?

AYN: Yes, Frank is my husband.

MARCEL: Mr. Rand?

AYN: Mr. O'Connor. I use my maiden name.

MARCEL: Ahh. *(Pause. He looks around himself.)* I can't believe that I am here.

AYN: Well you are. It is a reality. "A is A."

MARCEL: Yes, of course. It is a huge honour to meet you.

> *(He looks at the coffee table and spies a sculpture of a nude man, and is visibly shaken.)*

I'm afraid I'm very nervous.

AYN: You must not be. I understand that you are here because you value my ideas.

MARCEL: Well yes, that is—

AYN: There is no need to be nervous then. You value my ideas because you think there is some truth in them. That means you value me. Naturally that might cause you to be excited. I'm sure if you concentrate on your questions, on the reality before you, you will regain your confidence.

MARCEL: *(Looking away from the statue, focused.)* Thank you. First of all, may I say that you are a hero to me?

AYN: You may. But perhaps you should say … heroine.

> *(He expects her to dismiss the flattery. She looks at him calmly.)*

It is right that I should be a heroine to you, Mr. Pin. As you see, I have no use for false modesty. I have achieved much and I am proud of it. Why pretend otherwise?

MARCEL: You are exactly as I imagined you.

(She pulls out a long cigarette holder and lights a cigarette. While she has turned away MARCEL shifts the nude statue so the genitals no longer face him. She doesn't see this.)

AYN: Can I offer you a cigarette, Mr. Pin?

MARCEL: No, I don't smoke.

AYN: You should. It is one of life's few uncomplicated pleasures.

MARCEL: I have thought of trying but I don't think I would look very good … smoking.

AYN: What does it matter what others think?

MARCEL: Of course no, it doesn't matter. I'm sorry.

AYN: Don't apologize Mr. Pin. Just get to the point.

MARCEL: Mr. Pin. Get to the point. That's kind of funny …

AYN: Is it?

MARCEL: No, not really. *(He looks down, then up at her.)* Well, I—

AYN: *(Interrupting him.)* I understand you call yourself an Objectivist.

MARCEL: Well yes, I—

AYN: You mustn't—

MARCEL: But—

AYN: There are no Objectivists except for myself of course and perhaps—*(She softens slightly.)* perhaps one other. To be an objectivist is to see reality with a remarkable clarity. It is to live by reason, man's only means of survival in an irrational world. Most people are not capable of living by reason. Some try. I call those who try students of Objectivism. I presume that's what you are.

MARCEL: Well, yes, that's what I am then. A student of Objectivism.

AYN: And what questions do you have for me?

MARCEL: Well, first of all, as you can see, it's always been a problem for me that I well, I—one of my biggest questions is: I want very much to be like Howard Roark in your magnificent novel *The Fountainhead*. I want to be an independent person who thinks for himself but—

AYN: Well what's stopping you?

MARCEL: Well, I have always tried to think independently and to act independently. *(Shyly.)* I'm an artist, you see.

AYN: *(Interested.)* Ahh. What artistic endeavour are you engaged in, Mr. Pin?

MARCEL: I'm a … a florist.

(She stares at him blankly.)

I create … floral designs out of … of … *(He hesitates.)*

AYN: *(Finishing for him.)* Flowers. I see. *(Pause. She looks at him.)* Well there is nobility in every artistic endeavour. Now tell me why you can't live rationally. Why you can't be a hero like Howard Roark. I'm very interested.

MARCEL: Because well, because, life has not been very kind to me.

AYN: Life is unkind to all of us. That is no excuse.

MARCEL: It's not an excuse. I just … well I'd better just say it. This is a terrible problem. I couldn't think of anyone to help me, and then I thought of you.

AYN: I will do my best. But I can do nothing if you don't tell me the problem.

MARCEL: I know, it's embarrassing.

AYN: Stop apologizing. Howard Roark would never apologize.

(MARCEL stands up.)

MARCEL: You're right, of course, sorry. You see, the problem is, I've never been able to be the kind of man that you talk about in your novels because there's something that's stopping me. Something which is very embarrassing and horrible.

AYN: And irrational.

MARCEL: Yes, and irrational.

AYN: What is it.

MARCEL: Well I've never been able to function properly as a … as a man functions with women because well because when I was young a man … an older man, a neighbour, he—he assaulted me.

AYN: In what way.

(Pause.)

MARCEL: Physically. That is—

AYN: I see.

(Pause. He opens his mouth to say something else.)

Please don't say any more, Mr. Pin. I am not a psychotherapist. I am a philosopher. I am an epistemologist. But I am not qualified to—

MARCEL: I know, but what I was wondering was—

AYN: This man has acted irrationally. He has committed violence against you. That is why we have a police force. Did you call the police?

MARCEL: I was only a child.

AYN: Then you should call the police now.

MARCEL: But how will I ever prove that it happened.

AYN: You must try. It is the only way out of this horrible situation. *(She looks at her watch.)* Listen, Mr. Pin, I really must—

MARCEL: But I have to ask you, Miss Rand, I really have to ask you, if I am unable to convince the police that this man molested me, then what am I to do? The very existence of this man is offensive to me. The fact that he goes unpunished for his crimes is so irrational. He comes into my flower shop to this day. And I want ... I have these irrational desire about him.

AYN: Mr. Pin, I must insist—

MARCEL: Extreme irrational desires you see I ... *(He sits down on the piano bench.)* I sometimes feel that I want to harm him back, to defend myself sometimes even that ... that I want to ...

> *(He plays a single note on the piano, over and over again, staring down at the keys.)*

... kill him.

> *(He continues to play the note. She stands up and walks over to him to stop him.)*

AYN: Mr. Pin—

MARCEL: *(Still repeating the note.)* I have to admit I have ... I have the desire to kill him. And sometimes it's an uncontrollable desire, even when I try and think of other—

AYN: Stop. Mr. Pin. Stop. *(She stops him from playing and closes the piano.)* Listen to me. Let me tell you, I have been working with a very brilliant psychologist lately. In fact, I think he may be a genius, the genius in fact that we have all been waiting for. His name is Nathaniel Branden. This man is so brilliant that he may, indeed, one day be my intellectual heir. He has a private psychotherapy practice, where he treats everyday people. I will give you his card with his office address.

MARCEL: Why thank you Miss Rand. Thank you. I think I would like to see your therapist friend. I didn't think there was such a thing as an Objectivist therapist.

AYN: Before Nathaniel, there was not. But that has changed. *(She hands him a card.)* You may meet with him here.

MARCEL: Thank you. I don't know how I can ever thank you.

> *(He hugs her, she tries to wriggle free of his grasp.)*

AYN: You asked me for help. I gave it. There's no need to humiliate yourself over that simple fact.

> *(She walks him to the door. As she does so, the lights go to black in the living-room and come up just outside the apartment suite, in the hallway of the building. NATHANIEL and BARBARA BRANDEN stand there. NATHANIEL is a handsome young man of twenty-five and his wife BARBARA is blonde and young and very beautiful.)*

BARBARA: Nathan.

NATHAN: *(Annoyed.)* What?

> *(He raises his hand to knock on the door.)*

BARBARA: Before you knock. Can we talk about something?

NATHAN: You know how Ayn despises lateness.

BARBARA: I know, it's just—

> *(He turns on her. Holds her by the shoulders.)*

NATHAN: All right. Do you want to talk about one of those silly things or one of those serious things?

BARBARA: *(Flustered.)* I—I don't know.

NATHAN: Then, think. Is this going to be a rational discussion, which is based on carefully considered thought, or is it something related to your self-esteem.

BARBARA: I know the difference, Nathan.

NATHAN: Sometimes, I think you don't.

BARBARA: But sometimes, it's hard to analyze your feelings like that.

NATHAN: Well, think. I don't want to waste time this afternoon, dealing with issues that you should be dealing with in therapy.

BARBARA: I don't know what kind of a issue it is, but I—I just want to talk.

NATHAN: Barbara—

BARBARA: You make me nervous when you stand there with your hands on my shoulders like that.

NATHAN: So, you don't want me to touch you at all, now?

BARBARA: I didn't say that. Sometimes you twist things I say.

NATHAN: *(Taking out a cigarette.)* All right. What is it? What do you want to discuss?

BARBARA: It's not a big thing, I just wondered—well when I said I was feeling headachy you said this was a very important afternoon, and we shouldn't miss it.

NATHAN: I don't remember saying that.

BARBARA: Well you did.

NATHAN: So?

BARBARA: So what makes it so important?

NATHAN: Ayn might have said it was important. I can't remember.

BARBARA: *(Hopefully.)* Is she going to read us another chapter of *Atlas Shrugged?*

NATHAN: I don't know. I can't read her mind.

BARBARA: I just thought you might know.

NATHAN: Well I can't tell you for sure.

BARBARA: You can't or you won't?

NATHAN: *(Putting out his cigarette and grabbing her.)* Listen to me. You're being very irrational. The next thing you're going to tell me is that you've got a funny feeling—

BARBARA: Well I do—

NATHAN: *(Stamping around.)* Can't you see that is the worst kind of mysticism? Being ruled by your feelings? Can't you see that? What's next, tom toms and a voodoo spell? Or should we get a Ouija board and ask the God Moomoo if it's time to visit Ayn?

BARBARA: I'm not going in there.

(She walks away from the door. He follows her.)

NATHAN: Barbara. Listen to me—

BARBARA: No—

NATHAN: Barbara—

(They disappear down the hall. Lights come up on MARCEL, who is just about to reach the other side of the door, where he turns, suddenly, and walks from the tiny hall inside the apartment back into the living-room.)

MARCEL: Excuse me, Miss Rand. May I ask ask you one last thing?

AYN: Really, Mr. Pin, the daily demands upon my time are enormous. I am working on the final chapters of my next novel, and I'm expecting company—

MARCEL: Your next novel, how exciting—I was hoping you were working on another! What's it called?

AYN: *(Enjoying his interest, slightly.)* It is called *Atlas Shrugged.*

MARCEL: Oh, when will it be available?

AYN: Not for a very long time if you continue to ask me questions.

MARCEL: Oh just one more, Miss Rand, please, you are the only person who I respect in this world. Please. There are so few people of reason who one can respect.

> *(She sits down again, butting her cigarette and lighting another.)*

AYN: Go ahead.

MARCEL: Now I understand very much what you're saying about the police and how I should call them. That makes sense, and of course it would coming from you. But what I want to ask is this— it has nothing to do with emotion, that is—It is a philosophical question.

AYN: I am well prepared to answer such a question, Mr. Pin.

MARCEL: What I want to know is this. Philosophically speaking, what would be the right thing to do? This horrible man, he abused an innocent child in ways that the child does not wish to duscuss. Now the child understands that legally, that is, in the world of law and order, he should and would phone the police to deal with this matter. But the child cannot make himself even do that unless he believes in his heart of hearts that it is right that the man deserves to die. They may lock him up for life, you see, if the child can find proof. So for this man, it might be a sort of death in life. Do you feel that, logically speaking, the man deserves that death?

> *(AYN gets up. She paces about with her cigarette for a minute.)*

I realize I've asked you a very difficult question—

AYN: No. *(She waves him away.)* You have not.

> *(She paces some more. Then she turns on him, in a fury which is frightening.)*

Let me tell you a new word Mr. Pin. Have you ever heard of the word complicity?

MARCEL: Yes, I—

AYN: Well you know what it means. Then I will tell you a new word. Complicit. It is a word I have invented for those who collaborate with evil. That evil exists, that we cannot deny. We see it every day in the whimpering themes of Hollywood films and radio shows and now television. We see it in that glorification of what is truly the lowest of all common denominators: the common man. We see it in that celebration of mediocrity which we call our political system. We sit in the faces of all those who would squash ability and genius out of jealousy and fear. We see evil everywhere, and unless we smash it, unless we crush it, unless we grind it into the ground with every bit of human energy that we can muster, unless we live up to the highest ideal of ourselves, unless we live like a hero *every* single *day* of our lives we are nothing but complicit and we ourselves are *thieves* of life. There is no excuse for evil Mr. Pin. And if we do not do everything we can to kill it, then we are, ourselves, evil. *(She stares at him.)* Do you understand me Mr. Pin? It is terribly important that you absolutely understand what I am saying.

MARCEL: *(In her thrall.)* I understand. I understand.

> *(They are in a trance, for a moment; teacher and student.)*

AYN: Now Mr. Pin, you must go ahead and live your life as you see fit, according to the dictates of reason.

MARCEL: Yes, Miss Rand, thank you Miss Rand. How can I ever thank you?

> *(He suddenly kneels down and hugs her knees.)*

AYN: You may thank me by leaving now—*(She looks at her watch.)* or I may be late for my next appointment.

MARCEL: Yes, now I have the courage I need. I know that I am right.

AYN: Your reason will guide you.

MARCEL: Yes it will. Thank you. Thank you.

> *(She closes the door on him. She leans against the door, very tired. Lights fade on her and up on MARCEL's flower shop. It is a tiny space with a telephone and a desk and flowers everywhere. He runs in the door, out of breath.)*

Complicit, I must not be complicit, I must never be complicit. With evil. Never. Never. Thank you. Oh thank you Ayn Rand. Thank you for saving my life.

> *(He takes out a New York City phone book and thumbs through it.)*

Lever, Lever, Lever Brothers … Lever, Bruce, there.

> *(He picks up the phone and dials a number and waits for an answer.)*

Hello, is … *(His voice quivers.)* is ummm Bruce Lever there? Mr. Lever, hello, this is Marcel Pin. No, that is I think that you probably know me from Pin's flowers? Yes, it's a little flower shop, on Seventh Avenue. Yes, well I phoned you because I'm phoning all of my valued customers, to tell them about a special sale we have on Birds of Paradise ... yes ... that's the one ... yes, well how did I know it would be your very favorite flower? A florist's intuition I guess.

(He pulls the phone away from his mouth and whispers.)
Yes!!

(With a triumphant hand gesture. He goes back to the phone, confident, acting a little bit more like a homosexual.)

Well that's wonderful, I must save one for you. Or two? Two would be lovely. In the hall yes, they always look attractive in the hall, or under a mirror? *(Pause.)* How did I know you would have a mirror in the hall? Again, just call it florist's intuition I guess. So we shall see you later this afternoon, then. Goodbye Mr. Lever, nice talking to you. Goodbye.

(He hangs up the phone and reads out of his well-read copy of The Fountainhead.*)*

"Howard Roark stood naked at the edge of the cliff! ... His hair was neither blond nor red, but the exact colour of bright orange rind!" *(He holds the book close to him and kisses it.)* The hair. No ... I have to do my hair.

(He runs off. Lights dim on the flower shop. Lights up on the bright and very spacious living-room of Ayn and Frank. AYN stands smoking at the windows with her back to the room. FRANK enters quietly, and AYN speaks to him without even looking his way. He is wearing another lovely shirt.)

AYN: Ahh, you changed your shirt.

FRANK: For Nathaniel and Barbara.

AYN: I love this shirt Frank.

FRANK: I know you do, that's why I wore it. How was your student.

AYN: *(Sitting down with him.)* Well he thought he wasn't a student at all, he thought he was an Objectivist. *(She takes out a cigarette.)* He refused to smoke a cigarette with me, which I found very suspicious. He was inconsequential really.

FRANK: A second-hander?

AYN: A Peter Keating type—he lives through others. That kind of person can make you very depressed—a person of no value. It's horrible to think that there are people of no value at all living in the world.

FRANK: Perhaps the best thing to do is to concentrate on those who *do* have value.

AYN: Yes darling, of course. And that is what I will do. Actually this Mr. Pin—

FRANK: Such an odd name—

AYN: Yes, the name suits him, he's small and forgettable. Though not very sharp. A dull pin. This dull pin fits into that new category of souls that Nathaniel and I have been delineating, called emotionalists. I'm sure I've mentioned them to you before.

FRANK: Oh yes, of course, I remember. Now tell me, according to Nathaniel's theories, are emotionalists born or are they created?

AYN: That's a very relevant question. Nathaniel and I have defined two kinds of emotionalists. One kind of emotionalist are those people who are born that way. They are one step above the Peter Keatings, above those who depend completely on others to define their self-worth, but they are still almost hopeless. Then there are those who are emotionalists by default, that is, they become ruled by their emotions later in life due to an error of knowledge. These emotionalists are salvageable, thankfully.

FRANK: And Mr. Pin?

AYN: I fear he was born that way, or that he become an emotionalist early on, due to—an unfortunate traumatic experience. I gave him Nathaniel's card. If anyone can help him Nathaniel can.

FRANK: You have supreme faith in Nathaniel, don't you?

AYN: Yes, Frank, I think I could call that faith … supreme. And I think also that … well perhaps we should wait until Nathaniel and Barbara arrive before we discuss this.

FRANK: Certainly.

(There is a knock at the door.)

And there they are.

AYN: Frank.

FRANK: Yes?

AYN: Before you answer it, I want you to know something.

(She comes to him and holds his hands.)

FRANK: Yes.

AYN: You are my first love and my first true love, do you know that?

FRANK: Why, yes, you have said so many times.

AYN: And you will always, you will always be that very special one, do you understand?

FRANK: Of course, darling, of course.

(Another knock.)

You're acting very strangely. Was it the experience with Mr. Pin?

AYN: I think so. I think that's why.

(Another knock.)

Quickly, or they will knock down the door!

(She runs to the door in almost a schoolgirlish way, that we have not seen since the phone call at the beginning.)

Coming!

(She disappears into the tiny hallway. We hear her laughing good-natured voice offstage.)

Who is banging down my door here!

(She opens the front door. We hear some offstage talk—"A: How was your train ride? ... B: It was awful ... A: Oh that cannot be ... N: It's true!" as they put their coats away in the hall. Then we see her link arms with them and enter between NATHANIEL and BARBARA. AYN laughs with both, but leans slightly more towards NATHANIEL.)

I will not believe it. It cannot be ... you must be mistaken ... in your premises—

NATHAN: This is not a premise Ayn, this is a fact! Toot toot!

(He imitates a high and irritating train whistle. She laughs again with NATHANIEL.)

FRANK: *(Pleased to see her happy.)* What is it?

AYN: Nathaniel and Barbara say that they have had an awful train ride in from Connecticut. They say that the service was poor. And that the train stopped and started and it was not at all romantic. *(She imitates a high train whistle and laughs again.)* Toot toot!

FRANK: How can that be?

AYN: That's what I said to them. Train rides must always be wonderful, efficient, beautiful, romantic. Or—after my novel, they most certainly will be!

NATHAN: Toot!

(They all laugh. AYN is convulsed.)

AYN: *(As NATHANIEL and BARBARA sit down.)* Enough with the "toots"!

BARBARA: Are we going to hear another chapter of *Atlas Shrugged*? Is that why you've asked us here so specially today?

AYN: *(Breaking away from them, trying to compose herself.)* No. I'm still working on Galt's speech.

> *(BARBARA and NATHANIEL sit on the couch together.)*

BARBARA: What an incredibly long time you've spent working on that speech.

AYN: Ahh … but it must be the finest speech in the world. The finest speech ever written.

NATHAN: And it will be.

> *(He stares at her.)*

AYN: *(Staring back.)* Yes, I know that it will be.

BARBARA: I admire your incredible tenacity Ayn. That's why I don't think I could ever write a novel. A short story, maybe. I'm so eager to hear more. To hear you at the height of your powers as a writer. And, of course, I can't wait to meet John Galt.

AYN: What do you mean, my dear?

BARBARA: I mean I can't wait to read the novel for myself, when you're finished, and meet him as a real man, or as a real character.

AYN: *(Enjoying this; like the cat who ate the canary.)* But Barbara, you have met him.

BARBARA: That is—I mean when I really meet the character, by reading—

AYN: You have met the character, he is sitting beside you—

> *(FRANK smiles, thinking she is referring to him.)*

—on the couch.

> *(FRANK and BARABARA are shocked. NATHANIEL is embarassed.)*

BARBARA: *(Looking at NATHANIEL.)* I don't understand.

AYN: I mean, you are sitting beside John Galt.

BARBARA: Nathaniel?

AYN: Yes.

> *(BARBARA stares at her. FRANK looks disturbed. NATHANIEL looks a bit embarrassed.)*

BARBARA: But I thought you said that Frank was the basis for the character of John Galt.

AYN: I was wrong. Frank was the prototype. Nathaniel is the living man.

> *(They all relax a bit with this explanation. She and NATHANIEL stare at each other.)*

BARBARA: That's very … flattering.

AYN: No, it is not. It is simply the truth.

   (She lights a cigarette, and they all follow suit.)

   Barbara my dear.

BARBARA: Yes, Ayn.

AYN: I wanted to ask you what you your opinion of those records that I lent to you.

   (The tension in the room rises, they all stare at BARBARA.)

BARBARA: Yes.

AYN: So what did you think of them?

BARBARA: *(Slowly, carefully.)* Why they were all … lovely, I like music.

AYN: I know you do my dear. But I asked you to listen to three pieces of music. *(As if to a class.)* Do you all know the titles of the pieces that I lent to her?

FRANK: No, I don't.

AYN: You know their names, don't you, Nathaniel?

NATHAN: Saint-Saëns' *Second Piano Concerto*, Beethoven's *Third Symphony* and a Shostakovitch symphony, what was it—

AYN: Number two. Almost completely correct. Is that clear Frank?

FRANK: Yes.

AYN: So you must tell me what you thought of them dear. They are all vastly different types of music, written in different periods by composers with very different styles. Surely you did not love them all equally.

BARBARA: No, of course not. I should try and be more clear in my response.

AYN: Always be as clear as you can. It is the only way to deal with reality.

   (Pause; very tense again, they all stare at her.)

BARBARA: Well I … let me see, the Shostakovitch, was the very modern sounding one. Right, Nathan?

NATHAN: I'm sorry Barbara.

AYN: He is not going to help you. But in this case you are correct.

BARBARA: I found it … *(More tension. Again, slowly, carefully.)* I found it … interesting.

AYN: You did?

BARBARA: Yes.

AYN: Why?

BARBARA: Well it seemed to me that the music was experimenting in new ways with sound and with discordant ... it seemed like the music might have come from an independent mind.

AYN: I see. And the Beethoven. What did you think of that?

BARBARA: Well I thought ... *(She again is very tense, but feels that she might be succeeding.)* I felt it was brave and ... and heroic music. I felt that it expressed, or was attempting to express the possibilities of a heroic type of man.

AYN: Hence the subtitle.

(AYN and NATHANIEL laugh. FRANK smiles slightly.)

BARBARA: Pardon?

AYN: "Eroica" symphony.

BARBARA: *(Knowing she's been caught.)* I didn't know that was the subtitle.

AYN: *(Not sarcastically.)* Ahh, I see, you had not read the album cover. You wanted to keep an open mind. I can understand that. What about the third, the Saint-Saëns.

(Pause.)

BARBARA: Oh, I didn't care for that one.

AYN: You didn't?

BARBARA: No, I'm sorry, I didn't care for it at all.

(She looks around at FRANK and NATHANIEL who give her no support or help. They know this is a serious moment.)

AYN: Ahhh. Well then, Barbara, let me tell you a little bit about these composers, and their sense of life. You remember, we've talked before about the concept of a "sense of life."

BARBARA: Yes, of course I remember—

AYN: I'm afraid I don't agree with your analysis.

BARBARA: *(Frightened.)* You don't?

AYN: No. Let us start with Beethoven, which you said you admired. He is a classical composer credited with starting the romantic movement. But his music is ponderous and pretentious. There is no real joy in it. The Eroica symphony, which you so shrewdly perceived was about heroism—*(She suddenly turns very severe, snapping at her ruthlessly.)* I say shrewdly because you obviously had the foresight to read the album cover—despite your denials to the contrary—*(She calms down, and gets back to the subject at hand.)* this music is not moving at all. It would bore anyone with a true sense of the heroism of the human spirit.

BARBARA: But surely Ayn—

AYN: Excuse me, Barbara. I have not yet finished.

BARBARA: I'm sorry.

AYN: I forgive you. Let us move on to the Shostakovitch. I must confess that your analysis of the Shostakovitch is what confounds me most of all. You say that this music was composed by someone who has an independent mind, and you say that you admired it for its experimentation?

BARBARA: Well perhaps I should have said—

AYN: *(Very angry, ruthless again.) It is useless to imagine what you might have said, Barbara, you have already spoken* and I'm afraid that is what we must analyze here. *(She calms down and takes a philosophical tone.)* What we enjoy about music, if we enjoy anything at all, is the way that the chords have a logical sequence for the natural human response is a joy in order, in reason. This is why your response confounds me. How could you find joy in music which breaks all the rules of rational composition? What can possibly be the premises of a person who responds to confusion and illogic, instead of reason, to pain and discord instead of beauty?

NATHAN: Can I break in here, Ayn?

AYN: *(Sharply.)* If it's relevant.

NATHAN: I think all this is all particularly relevant to a psychological theory I am developing. If a person finds joy in disorder, for instance, then it means that a person has a psychological problem based on a false premise. They value disorder. Somewhere, subconsciously as a child, through the irrational actions of the parents, they have been taught to value irrationality.

AYN: Nathan, I cannot believe that anyone actually values the irrational, the chaotic.

NATHAN: But of course they do.

AYN: Consciously?

NATHAN: Not necessarily.

AYN: But that is so evil.

NATHAN: Sometimes I think you are too much of an optimist. Sometimes I think you can't come to terms with the true horror of the world's stupidity.

AYN: You may be right. Nathan. Now, may I continue with my analysis?

NATHAN: I'm devouring your every word.

AYN: I hadn't thought of my words as a tasty dinner, but I will accept the metaphor—

(They all laugh at this little joke, even BARBARA.)

—coming from you. Now, I hesitate to formulate a final conclusion about your ideas, Barbara, until I have responded to your final choice. Let us talk about your response to the Saint-Saëns *Second Piano Concerto.*

(BARBARA looks at her, hopefully, unaware somehow that she is still to be attacked viciously if she attempts to interrupt.)

I will have to say that here, I agreed with you, somewhat.

(BARBARA brightens up.)

But unfortunately, it is here also that you have made your most grievous error. It is true that the first and last movements of this concerto fall short of Rachmaninoff's *Second Piano Concerto*, which portrays man at his best, at his finest. But let us talk about the second movement, Barbara. The second movement of the Saint-Saëns.

BARBARA: You know, I forgot to say that—

AYN: *(Snapping at her again, very angry.) Do not tell me that you have forgotten anything!! If you did not have the presence of mind to tell me your complete response then I fear not only for yor sense of life but for your basic intelligence ... (She softens, touches her shoulder.)* No, I think you are an intelligent woman, Barbara, but your premises are at best confused, and at worse, fundamentally evil. The second movement of Saint-Saëns' *Second Piano Concerto* is one of the most heart-wrenchingly joyous pieces of music ever written. Its light-hearted sense of life was one of the few things that helped me through the drudgery of my dreadful tortured existence in my nightmare days in Soviet Russia. And how you somehow missed this heaven on Earth that the composer created—

BARBARA: I'm sorry Ayn—

AYN: *(Snapping again.) There is no point in apologizing!!* Barbara, you could not possibly have responded to this music in this way unless there was something fundamentally wrong with your sense of life, and therefore your basic premises. Nathaniel has told me that he has asked you many times to consider therapy with him and countless times you have refused. Let me tell you something

Barbara: you ignore his generous invitations at your psychological peril. You are a person with a vacant and vacuous and perhaps a diseased and perhaps even evil sense of life.

BARBARA: *(Carefully.)* But surely, Ayn, it might just be a matter of taste—

>   *(FRANK and NATHANIEL look at AYN, knowing the tirade to come.)*

AYN: You talk to me of taste? Of *taste?!* *(Then fiercely—a tirade.)* Are you an animal?! Are you nothing but a lizard or a dinosaur or some amoeba that slides around in the muck smelling of disease—revelling in the stench of garbage and human waste?! Don't speak to me of taste!! An animal has taste!! An animal arises in the morning and satisfies its bodily functions!! But you Barbara I hope are still human. I hope you can exercise your mind. Please don't talk to me of taste ever again, Barbara, please. It disgusts me!!

BARBARA: Yes Ayn. I'm sorry Ayn.

>   *(Pause. AYN winces at her apology.)*

AYN: Don't be sorry. Get it fixed! *(Pause.)* I think we should all have some tea now, after our discussion. Frank has made us some of his famous peppermint tea. Frank?

FRANK: Yes, Ayn.

>   *(FRANK disappears.)*

AYN: *(Sitting down and lighting another cigarette.)* So, Nathaniel, I have another patient for you. Besides Barbara, who will soon be knocking on your therapeutic door, I think.

NATHAN: If you keep bringing me patients, I will be the busiest therapist in New York City.

AYN: And what's wrong with that? You are the best.

BARBARA: Excuse me, Ayn, I'm feeling a headache coming on, do you mind if I get an aspirin?

AYN: *(Very motherly and solicitous.)* Of course not dear. Go right ahead. *(She points out the door and down the hall, holding her arm.)* You know where the cabinet is, down the hall and turn left, yes—*(To NATHANIEL.)* He is a florist named *Pin*, who refuses to smoke. If he says that I recommended him, then he is not lying … *(She watches for BARBARA's exit, then suddenly in hushed tones.)* Oh my darling. *(She sits and holds his hand passionately.)* Now that we have discussed Barbara's false premises, now is the time …

NATHAN: I didn't think that we had fully decided, on the phone …

AYN: Are you wavering, my love?

NATHAN: No, of course not—

AYN: It was our telephone call this afternoon, that made me realize that I couldn't wait any longer. How can you?

NATHAN: *(Grabbing her with an animal growl.)* Oh Ayn.

> *(They kiss. Lights fade on the scene and come up on the florist shop. Very cramped but very bright. MARCEL sits behind the counter, reading* The Fountainhead. *His hair has been dyed the exact colour of ripe orange rind. A dinging noise and the door opens. It is BRUCE LEVER—a homosexual in his mid-thirties. He is as out of the closet as a man might be in 1955. He wears an ascot and a flowered shirt and casual slacks and sports shoes and is a bit effeminate. But he is not sleazy or excessively flirtatious. In fact he is quite cheerful, honest, and matter-of-fact. He walks up to the counter. MARCEL quickly hides his book.)*

BRUCE: Hello.

MARCEL: Hi.

BRUCE: I'm Bruce Lever.

MARCEL: I thought you were.

BRUCE: *(Smiling.)* How did you know?

MARCEL: I think it was … the shirt.

BRUCE: Well I thought … a flower shop, a coloured shirt. Why not?

MARCEL: *(Carefully.)* It was just a whim, then. Do you have … lots of whims?

BRUCE: Why yes, I do actually. I think.

> *(Pause.)*

MARCEL: And do you always follow them?

BRUCE: I try as best as I can. I guess you could call me whimsical. *(Pause, then matter-of-factly.)* As well as musical. *(Pause.)* If you know what I mean.

MARCEL: *(He doesn't.)* I *think* I do.

BRUCE: Why all these questions?

MARCEL: *(Staring at him.)* I find you … interesting.

BRUCE: *(Surprised, but cheerfully complying.)* Well I find you … interesting too. *(BRUCE stares at him.)* Pardon me for asking but … did you change your hair?

MARCEL: Yes I did. *(Pause.)* Do you like it?

BRUCE: *(Checks him out.)* It suits you.

MARCEL: Why thank you.

BRUCE: The colour is very … bold.

MARCEL: *(Flirting, but controlling his disgust.)* Sometimes I can be very … bold, too.

BRUCE: Ahh … *(He clears his throat.)* You said that you had a special today on Bird of Paradise flowers?

MARCEL: Why yes we do. *(He pulls some flowers out.)* They are on special for $5.99 for the pair.

BRUCE: How lovely to have, a pair.

MARCEL: Yes.

BRUCE: Two are always better than one.

MARCEL: So they say.

BRUCE: I'll take them.

MARCEL: Can I ask you, why you are so fond of this particular flower?

BRUCE: I don't know.

MARCEL: Another whim?

BRUCE: Yes, I suppose.

> *(Pause. He counts out his money. BRUCE gathers his courage.)*

No, that's not true. I think I love this flower because … may I be honest with you?

MARCEL: Yes, please do.

BRUCE: I love this flower because … because … it reminds me of something very special, of … *(He lowers his voice.)* of the slender, delicate, arch of the neck of a boy.

MARCEL: Ahh.

> *(MARCEL is speechless. He hands him the flowers. BRUCE hands him the money which he doesn't want to touch.)*

Why thank you Mr. Lever, for taking advantage of our sale.

BRUCE: You're quite welcome. *(He turns to go.)*

MARCEL: *(Suddenly blurting it out.)* Do you have any plans for this evening?

BRUCE: Why no, as a matter of fact, I don't think I do.

MARCEL: I was thinking that you might like to go for … a walk.

BRUCE: What a lovely idea.

MARCEL: It's going to be a very warm night—*(He does what he imagines is a slightly gay gesture.)* and it occurred to *(Being very fey.) moi*—to go for a walk by the Hudson River. You know where it gets up high, and there's a view.

BRUCE: Well, that would be very nice.

MARCEL: *(Too quickly.)* Do you want to meet me around nine p.m. at the end of 107th Street just past Tenth Avenue?

BRUCE: *(Surprised, but pleased.)* I'd like that very much.

MARCEL: Okay well *(Again trying to act gay.)* we'll … see you there.

BRUCE: Thank you Mr. Pin.

MARCEL: Call me Marcel.

BRUCE: *(Warming.)* Marcel. See you later.

> *(He turns and walks out of the shop, but stops at the door.)*

Oh, Marcel.

MARCEL: Yes?

BRUCE: I just have to ask you something. It's just been, it's been driving me crazy since I walked in.

MARCEL: *(Frightened.)* Yes.

BRUCE: You just … it's nuts but … you remind me of someone … I can't place who or where …

MARCEL: Do I?

BRUCE: Yes … it's maddening.

MARCEL: Well you've been coming in here to shop on and off for about a year … maybe it's that.

BRUCE: Oh well … *(He points his finger trying to place him.)* It's just … you're probably right. *(His finger falls.)* It's probably just the hair colour.

> *(He exits again. MARCEL has put on rubber gloves and is trying to dispose of the Bird of Paradise flowers that BRUCE touched and defiled. He is caught by BRUCE.)*

Oh Marcel, so, after all this time, what made you invite me for a walk? *(Pause.)* Was it the colourful shirt?

MARCEL: Maybe … Oh maybe just … call it a whim …

BRUCE: A whim is a desire that has no reason.

MARCEL: That's me … *(Trying to be fey again.)* whimsical!

BRUCE: *(He looks at MARCEL warmly.)* See you later, Marcel. *(He holds up the flowers in salute.)* To our whims!

(He walks out of the flower shop, gaily. MARCEL waits for him to go and then pulls the heads off the Bird of Paradise display flowers, angrily.)

MARCEL: He doesn't recognize me. Of course he doesn't recognize me. I was a child … a little boy. With a delicate arched neck. *(He writes in his copy of* The Fountainhead.*)* Yes … a second-hander, Ayn was so right … a definite second-hander of the most evil kind! Yes!

(He scribbles as the lights dim. Lights up on Ayn and Frank's apartment. FRANK can be heard in the other room handling teacups. BARBARA has not yet returned from the bathroom. This scene begins where the last left off.)

AYN: We must tell them now.

NATHAN: Yes we must.

AYN: Then I will start.

NATHAN: As we agreed.

AYN: This is so thrilling! It's like something from a novel.

NATHAN: It's the way life always should be.

(As FRANK enters with tea, AYN changes her tone to something more formal.)

AYN: Nathaniel, have you ever met a man of perfect psychology?

NATHAN: You know, I can't say that I have. Except for Frank, of course.

AYN: Yes, of course I was excepting ourselves from the question.

NATHAN: You know, I think it's one of the pervasive influences of our morally corrupt culture.

AYN: You mean the culture of altruism effects people's psychology?

NATHAN: Most definitely yes. It cripples people emotionally. You know, Ayn I've been thinking.

AYN: That's certainly no surprise. *(She takes some tea and continues to talk to NATHAN, ignoring FRANK.)* And what have you been thinking?

NATHAN: How important an objective psychotherapy is to people in our culture. How much people *need* a rational therapist. Especially those who read your novels. You know, I wish I could help all the people who read your novels to reach out directly to you, and get help.

AYN: Oh, but Nathan, I wouldn't want them to.

FRANK: There was a horrible man this morning—

AYN: Excuse me, Frank, sorry darling—*(To NATHAN.)* and I don't *give* help. You know that. I respond to the best in people. I don't *help.*

NATHAN: I understand that. I used the wrong word. Those people who value your novels, would also value reasoned psychotherapy.

FRANK: Like that little man.

NATHAN: Who was this ... little man?

AYN: Inconsequential ... Came to me for advice.

NATHAN: What was his problem?

AYN: Oh dear, I don't want to talk about it. He depressed me. I gave him your office address. Really Frank, I don't know how he does it.

FRANK: What.

NATHAN: You mean psychotherapy?

AYN: I really don't know how you deal with all those emotional cripples. *(She shudders.)* I don't have the stomach for it. It would drive me crazy.

NATHAN: Someone has to deal with it.

AYN: I suppose they must.

NATHAN: Don't underestimate me, Ayn.

AYN: How can you say that? I just called you the living hero of my work. How can you even think I don't respect you totally in every way?

NATHAN: How can you think that I might be unable to deal with emotional cripples? Human psychology is my job. It's my passion. You may not completely understand that passion, but that's because it's my territory—just as literature and philosophy are yours.

AYN: *(Always amazed by him.)* Of course my dear, you are right.

> *(BARBARA arrives from the bathroom. AYN is again, very solicitous.)*

Barbara, my dear, welcome back. So how's the headache? Are you feeling better?

BARBARA: Yes, much, thank you.

> *(She sits down on a chair facing AYN and NATHANIEL, who are on the couch. FRANK also faces the couch.)*

AYN: We're about to enjoy Frank's special peppermint tea. Would you like some?

BARBARA: Yes please.

AYN: I'll admit I'll take a good cup of coffee any day, but Frank finds this soothing, so we drink it for him.

(They all sip their tea, with AYN leading the toast. This is a ritual. They finish their sip and look at each other approvingly.)

BARBARA: Mmmm.

NATHAN: Delicious.

AYN: That hits the spot. *(Pause.)* So. Barbara, Frank—Nathaniel and I have something which we would like to discuss with you.

BARBARA: *(Placing down her cup.)* Nathaniel, you didn't tell me that.

NATHAN: I must have forgotten.

BARBARA: I don't like surprises. *(She turns to AYN.)* I remember once you told me you didn't like surprises, Ayn. You told me they were irrational.

AYN: Now Nathaniel, you should have told Barbara. You should have warned her. But there's nothing we can do about it now. I would have warned Frank, but he's my rock … and I know that nothing, not even a surprise will unsettle him. *(Seated, she has lit a cigarette.)* So, there is something that Nathaniel and I have to tell you. As both of you may have noticed, over the past four years that Nathaniel and I have known each other, we have had a teacher–student relationship which has been more than inspirational. That is, certainly our relationship started out as one between teacher and student, but gradually, it has developed into something else, something more than just well, scholastic. Now I know that the two of you will understand—because, well you know what I am, and you know what Nathan is. We are two people whose lives are ruled by reason. We are ruthless in our application of our intellects. I'm sure you can imagine what incredible pleasure it is for us to exchange ideas and exercise that reason. You are both very intelligent people also, and I'm sure you can understand the pure joy of finding an intellectual equal. As you know from my philosophy, romantic love is a logical thing. One loves the person who is the highest value. So I'm sure you will understand, that due to our very natures, Nathan and I have found that, well, that we love each other.

(Pause. The room is still. AYN picks up the tea and takes a calm sip.)

Mmmm. That's delicious, Frank. *(She carefully puts her cup down and resumes her speech again.)* And I want to be clear about this. That love is not purely pedantic or purely Platonic, if I may use an adjective which I detest. No, this love is romantic. It is the love of a man for a woman and a woman for a man.

(Pause. They again are silent.)

And I know that you are rational people who will not let their emotions rule them at this critical moment. I know that you will be able to understand and tolerate, no, more than tolerate, that you will be able to respect this love what we have. It does not affect my love for you, Frank, or Nathan's love for Barbara. It is a response to excellence, to intelligence and brilliance. It is the highest of all human responses. *Of course* we still love both of you, but we wanted you to know that we also love each other.

(An incredibly long pause. Then BARBARA drops her tea.)

BARBARA: *(Staring down at the mess.)* Oh.

AYN: Oh, Frank, Barbara seems have dropped her tea, could you—

BARBARA: No. Please. I'll blot it out with this. *(She takes out a handkerchief.)* It's only Frank's peppermint tea, after all. It's not liable to stain. *(As she blots, she speaks, hazily.)* I … I don't understand.

(Pause.)

AYN: Should I explain it again?

FRANK: *(Staring levelly at her.)* Yes.

AYN: I'm saying that Nathaniel and I love each other.

BARBARA: But there's a difference between love and … being … in love. *(She steels herself.)* Are you saying that you are in love with my husband?

AYN: Yes, and he is in love with me.

BARBARA: Is this true, Nathan?

NATHAN: Yes.

BARBARA: I don't understand. How can you say that to me?

NATHAN: We just want to be completely honest.

(Pause. They all look at each other for a moment. NATHANIEL is not able to look at FRANK. Then BARBARA bursts out.)

BARBARA: And you expect us to accept it? *(She stands up, very angry.)* That is barbaric!!

AYN: Barbara, you are not acting reasonably.

BARBARA: I am not acting reasonably? You tell me that you want to have an affair with my husband and then you tell me that I if I am angry I am not acting reasonably? Well Nathan happens to be of value to me to, and we also happen to be married! Something which we are painfully aware of—since you were my maiden of honour!

AYN: Barbara please, I ask you to think before you speak—

BARBARA: I have *thought*. As soon as you started to speak about teacher and student I had a feeling about what you were going to say—

AYN: There, you see—a *feeling!!*

BARBARA: And then I had a *thought* and that thought was no. This is impossible. I will not be reasonable about my husband having an affair with another woman.

FRANK: You're asking a lot Ayn. Maybe too much.

AYN: I don't think so Frank. Not if you understand completely.

BARBARA: What don't we understand?

AYN: No one said anything about an affair. About a physical affair..

BARBARA: But you said it was a romantic love.

AYN: Yes, it is. But, Nathan—can you speak for a moment please?

NATHAN: Yes. *(He sits up, ready with his rehearsed argument.)* What Ayn and I wanted to suggest is this. We have discussed this endlessly and we think that we have a plan that would be rational and acceptable for everyone. We suggest that Ayn and I have private visits with each other, for three hours twice a week, and that, well that we simply be allowed to have that private time together. *(Pause.)* That's all.

FRANK: For … what reason.

NATHAN: Because we value each other. And we would like to be together.

FRANK: As man and wife?

NATHAN: Ayn is your wife, not mine.

(Pause.)

BARBARA: But I don't understand—if you value each other, and you love each other as two reasonable people, wouldn't you want to … have complete intimacy?

AYN: We also value the two of you, Barbara. I love Frank and Nathan will always love you. Because of that love, that value, we agree not to be intimate with each other. All we want is that time to be together, privately.

BARBARA: But you are already, alone—working—

AYN: But we won't be working. We'll be loving each other. You see, we didn't want to sneak around and lie. We love you both and value you both and we wanted you to know the truth. *(Pause.)* And we both hope that you can be as reasonable with us as we are being with you.

BARBARA: I don't know …

> *(Pause. The room is very silent.)*

You say the two of you won't be intimate?

AYN: We will not be doing … that.

BARBARA: Nathaniel?

NATHAN: No. We will not be … doing that.

BARBARA: I don't know. I—*(Pause. She looks at FRANK.)* What do you think, Frank?

FRANK: I think … I think … *(Pause.)* I think I need to collect my thoughts. *(He gets up.)* Barbara. Would you like to go for a walk?

BARBARA: Well I … I don't know. I don't know what I'd like.

NATHAN: Maybe I should take you home—

BARBARA: *(Quickly fiercely.) No I* … no. Sorry. I don't want to go home right now. I just want to clear my head. *(She looks at FRANK.)* All right. Let's go for a walk …

FRANK: Okay. *(He turns to AYN.)* You certainly can't expect us to make a decision all of a sudden, today, sitting here in this room. Barbara and I have similar decisions to make. Maybe we should have a talk about all this—*(He looks at AYN sharply.)* perhaps there are some things Barbara and I can learn from each other, if we talk.

BARBARA: *(Looking defiantly at NATHANIEL and AYN.)* Well all right then … let's go.

> *(FRANK gets their coats and they go towards the door..)*

I just need to clear my head, that's all, it's so stuffy in here …

> *(He gives her a coat. She turns to NATHANIEL suddenly at the door, and speaks almost dreamily.)*

I don't want to leave you alone with her right now.

AYN: *(Aghast.)* Barbara.

NATHAN: *Barbara.* Please. If you want to go home.

BARBARA: *No!! (Pause.)* I mean … I don't want to go home.

NATHAN: Well then we'll talk later.

BARBARA: Yes, we'll do that.

FRANK: *(Looking at AYN again.)* Wish us luck.

AYN: Goodbye my darling.

FRANK: Goodbye. *(To BARBARA.)* So, shall we go?

BARBARA: Yes, I—

> *(They move towards the door together.)*

But there's still something I don't understand. You said that ... you said that you—*(She almost starts to cry.)* you loved each other and ... it was romantic love—doesn't that mean—

NATHAN: Barbara please. For God's sake—*(He turns with an aside to AYN.)* And you know Ayn, that I call on God out of habit, not because I believe in him—*(He rushes over to BARBARA and puts his hands on her shoulders.)* For God's sake Barbara, we've had the honesty and decency to come and talk to you about this. Do you think that we would be this honest with you and then go and be intimate behind your backs? What do you think we are, animals? We are the two most rational people you will ever know. Surely you understand that.

BARBARA: *(Still dazed.)* Yes, I do.

FRANK: Let's go Barbara. *(He puts his arm around her waist and turns to AYN.)* We'll be back in about an hour.

BARBARA: Goodbye Nathaniel. Goodbye Ayn.

NATHAN: Goodbye Barbara.

AYN: Goodbye. *(Pause.)* Thank you, Frank darling.

> *(He says nothing to her, but walks out the door. The room is darker. After they have gone, AYN stands at the doorway with her back to NATHANIEL.)*

My darling Nathan, my darling, you are my everything, you are my highest ideal, you are my every wish, you are my every whim, you give me permission to be a woman. *(She walks over to him.)* What is it you want of me my darling? *(She takes a hold of his shoulders, and kisses his neck.)* Oh yes ... yes do whatever you wish. I am yours I am yours forever. Use me, I am here for your use. *(She slides down his body to the floor at his feet.)* Treat me in any manner you wish. I am at your feet, I am nothing. You are my perfect man do to me whatever please whatever you will ...

> *(She cries and hugs his legs. The lights dim to black.)*
>
> *End of Act One.)*

Act Two

(Lights up on a cliff over the Hudson River. It is dusk. There is a tree next to the edge of the cliff. MARCEL and BRUCE are having a picnic.)

MARCEL: It's nice of you to bring sandwiches.

BRUCE: I thought you might like them.

MARCEL: What's in them? *(He looks inside.)* Is it cucumbers?

BRUCE: Yes. Cucumbers.

MARCEL: That's a strange thing to put in a sandwich.

BRUCE: Haven't you ever seen *The Importance of Being Earnest?*

MARCEL: I can't say that I have.

BRUCE: Well these were Oscar Wilde's favorite sandwiches.

(Suddenly MARCEL finds the sandwich inedible.)

MARCEL: You mean … the famous homo—*(He has trouble saying the word.)*

BRUCE: —sexual? Why yes. *(Pause.)* But of course he's also remembered for other things.

MARCEL: Like what?

BRUCE: Like writing plays and poems and … well just being an all 'round talented person.

MARCEL: Oh, I thought everyone always remember him for being a homo—*(He still can't finish the word.)*

BRUCE: —sexual. Well there's that too.

(Pause. MARCEL puts down what's left of his sandwich.)

I hope you don't mind me saying, you're a very different sort of boy—in some ways.

MARCEL: What ways?

BRUCE: Well, you don't seem, again—I hope you don't mind me saying this—well some people might take this as a compliment but—

MARCEL: What.

BRUCE: Some people might not know right off that you're—well a homosexual.

MARCEL: They wouldn't?

BRUCE: You see, I try and give a few hints. Like you, I work in the arts—I do window design—and I'm certainly not afraid if people get a hint. Sometimes it can get me into trouble—but the right kind of trouble if you know what I mean.

MARCEL: *(Amazed and horrified but not showing it.)* Uh-huh. Well maybe the reason people don't know that I'm a homosexual right away is because I'm not.

BRUCE: You're not?

MARCEL: No.

BRUCE: You're not a homosexual?

MARCEL: No.

BRUCE: Oh. That's strange. I mean I can usually read all the signs. You sure seemed very musical to me.

MARCEL: *(Frustrated.)* Musical?

BRUCE: Yes. Musical. It's a term that means ... homosexual.

MARCEL: Oh. *(Pause.)* I see.

> *(Pause. He has to take a rest from all this. He stands up with his back to BRUCE.)*

Nice night, isn't it.

BRUCE: It's beautiful.

MARCEL: I love clear nights like this, when you can see everything down below.

BRUCE: Yes, this is a prime spot. *(Pause. BRUCE stares at him.)* Marcel, I hope you don't mind me asking. If you're not a ... friend of Dorothy, then why would you want to—well—

MARCEL: A friend of what?

BRUCE: If you're not ... musical.

MARCEL: Oh yeah, musical. *(Pause.)* Why would I want to what?

BRUCE: If you're not musical, well why would you want to ... well go for a walk with me?

MARCEL: Well ... I guess I should tell you ... gee. *(He sits down again, trying to be cordial and hide his disgust.)* These cucumber sandwiches can really grow on you. *(He takes another but puts lots of mustard on it.)* I guess I should tell you that when you thought you recognized me from somewhere in the store you were right. You do know me. In a way.

BRUCE: I do?

MARCEL: Yes. My mother got married a second time. When I was little, people used to call me Marc. Marc DayRubay.

BRUCE: Oh my God!

(*Pause. MARCEL watches him eagerly.*)

Little Marc DayRubay—I don't believe it! (*Pause.*) You used to live next door to me! (*Pause. He contemplates the past.*) God when I knew you you, were just—

MARCEL: Thirteen years old.

BRUCE: I never would have recognized you.

MARCEL: (*Ironically.*) I've grown eh?

BRUCE: Well that was … it must have been thirteen years ago. I was barely twenty. (*Pause.*) I remember, I used to take swims in your pool.

MARCEL: Yeah.

BRUCE: Well what a coincidence, you working at the flower shop and everything I mean.

MARCEL: Life is full of coincidences.

BRUCE: But I would for sure have taken you for being musical.

MARCEL: Well, I'm not.

BRUCE: Wow. Wow. What a coincidence. And you knew all the time?

MARCEL: Yeah, I knew.

BRUCE: Why didn't you tell me?

MARCEL: I wanted to surprise you.

BRUCE: You're a mischievous little guy aren't you?

MARCEL: Sometimes.

BRUCE: Have you got the mustard?

MARCEL: Here.

(*MARCEL hands him some.*)

BRUCE: But wait a minute. (*Spreading the mustard thoughtfully.*) If you don't mind me asking … didn't we … didn't we … fool around?

MARCEL: *Fool around?*

BRUCE: Yes. Didn't we … you know … when we were kids … *(Pause. He smiles, but not lasciviously.)* diddle each other or something?

MARCEL: *(Getting very angry at him.)* Did we?

BRUCE: I may be wrong, I can't remember everything I did. I mean I was a pretty crazy teenager. Almost a juvenile delinquent.

MARCEL: You were an adult to me.

BRUCE: I may have looked adult to you, but I was just a kid.

MARCEL: *(Very piqued.)* You looked completely adult to me.

BRUCE: Okay. *(Noticing his pique but not letting it faze him.)* I guess I did. *(Pause.)* Didn't you ask me some pretty … hot questions? Wasn't that how it started?

> *(MARCEL stares at him, furious. BRUCE smiles at him, sweetly, openly.)*

Didn't we … do some diddling?

> *(Pause.)*

MARCEL: I seem to remember that … *(Pause. He stares at BRUCE.)* that there was some diddling or other going on. Someone was diddling somebody. As I remember. *(He laughs, strangely.)* I mean someone was doing some *diddling* Bruce. That's for sure!

> *(He laughs wildly, angrily. Pause. BRUCE stares at him.)*

BRUCE: Are you okay Marc?

MARCEL: *(Screaming at him.)* Call me Marcel!

BRUCE: Marcel.

> *(Pause.)*

MARCEL: I prefer that, now that I'm grown up now too.

BRUCE: *(Staring at him, disturbed.)* No really, are you okay?

MARCEL: *(Brightly.)* Sure.

BRUCE: You're acting very strangely.

MARCEL: Am I? Sorry. I guess it's the cucumber sandwiches. They give me the giggles.

> *(He laughs. They sit and eat in silence for a minute.)*

Are those Fig Newtons?

BRUCE: Yeah.

MARCEL: My favorite. They might calm me down.

> *(BRUCE gives him one.)*

Thanks.

> *(They munch in silence for a minute. BRUCE watches MARCEL.)*

BRUCE: So let me get this straight, you're not musical, but you invited me up here to have a chat about old times when we were kids?

MARCEL: I guess. And I wanted to look at the view, you know?

BRUCE: Oh. It is a great view.

MARCEL: Thanks for the picnic Bruce. I think I'm full though. Better stretch my legs.

BRUCE: Yeah, I know what you mean.

(BRUCE packs things up. MARCEL has freaked him out.)

MARCEL: *(Standing by the cliff.) Wow,* what a fantastic view from up here.

(He puts his hand on the tree by the cliff to steady himself.)

BRUCE: Yeah, it's great up here.

MARCEL: Bruce come here. I want you to have a look at the view.

(BRUCE stares at him. The lights dim to black.

Lights up on Ayn and Frank's apartment. This scene begins slightly later than the conclusion of Act One. They are kissing on the couch, their legs intertwined. They are both moaning. Then he moves away. He kisses her gently on the cheek and nestles back, reaching for a cigarette. This is not necessarily abrupt, but it seems so to AYN.)

AYN: *(Sitting up.)* Nathan, what's wrong?

NATHAN: *(Caressing her cheek.)* Nothing.

AYN: But I don't understand. Why are we …

NATHAN: What?

AYN: Well I … I have to … I have to talk to you. Cigarette—

NATHAN: Certainly. *(He gives her one.)*

AYN: I … I'm sorry Nathaniel but you … this is very difficult for me.

NATHAN: Darling, you can say anything to me.

AYN: I know … I know … But it's difficult, with my upbringing, to talk about things like this. *(She kisses him.)* Darling you … you aren't—you aren't acting like a man with me.

NATHAN: *(Caressing her again.)* I don't know what you mean.

AYN: You know what I mean. *This is so frustrating. (She kisses him on the cheek again.)* I'm sorry darling. I'm new to this kind of openness, but I know that I can trust you. Especially a psycho-therapist.

NATHAN: Now, now. A therapist. I don't have my degree yet.

AYN: I know. The thing is, Nathaniel ... You won't laugh at me, will you?

NATHAN: Of course I won't laugh at you. I love you. You are my highest value.

AYN: I know. I just think that you aren't ... that you aren't expressing your love the way a man usually expresses his love ... for a woman.

NATHAN: My darling, I don't understand exactly what you mean.

AYN: *(Suddenly.)* Oh Nathan—*please don't be naive.*

NATHAN: I'm not being naive, I mean I'm trying not to be—

AYN: I really don't want to say the words. We have been passionately kissing each other and showing our love for each other as two equals. And yet you have never once—a woman knows these things—you have never once shown me well ... the proof of your desire. *(Standing up, snapping at him with her back to him.) Now do you know what I mean?!*

NATHAN: Not really.

AYN: *Oh Christ!!*

NATHAN: Darling, tell me what you're talking about—

AYN: I don't want to say these words, for God's sake Nathan—and I use the Lord's name as you know, just out of habit and frustration for I am most certainly not a theist—for God's sake Nathan all right there has not been for me, for the woman you value, there has not been—I can't say it. I *can't* say it. *(Pause.)* Oh. I cannot believe that I have had to speak these vague and despicable words to you, my perfect man.

NATHAN: *(Gently.)* Ayn, listen. Sometimes lovers they ... well you know they have to talk things out. *(Pause.)* Don't you and Frank ever talk about—

AYN: Never. There's no need to talk about things like that with him. He's always ... perfect. In fact, a man must always be ... perfect with the woman he loves. And you ... a man of youth and vigour,

(She is revving up; he observes her calmly, as if he has a secret weapon.)

NATHAN: Ayn, please. Sit down—

AYN: I won't sit down! Well maybe there is a problem here. Because there is something wrong here, there is something seriously wrong with your premises *Mister* if you cannot respond if you will not respond to your highest value.

NATHAN: Listen to me. Calm down Ayn ... please ...

AYN: I am reacting reasonably—

NATHAN: No, you're not.

AYN: *Do not tell me I'm being irrational. Am I not your highest value?!*

NATHAN: Of course, Ayn—

AYN: *Am I not the perfect woman of reason that you love?!*

NATHAN: Yes of course—

AYN: *Then check your premises young man!! (Then, fiercely.)* Would you prefer a whore then?! Is that what you would prefer?! I hope I sincerely hope that this has nothing to do with the fact that I am a few years older than you, I hope it has nothing to do with that!! Let me tell you if I was dying and in a wheelchair and my body was covered with scabs you should still have desire for me. Why?! Why?! Because I am your highest value.

NATHAN: Listen to me.

> *(He moves towards her.)*

AYN: No.

NATHAN: Listen.

AYN: No.

> *(There is a pause. He slaps her. She screams in pain and touches her face, but her anger is immediately quelled. She looks at him lustfully. He grabs her.)*

NATHAN: Listen to me—Ayneleh.

AYN: *(Hazily, confused.)* How did you know that? How did you know to call me that?

NATHAN: You'd be surprised what I know ...

AYN: It's what my father used to call me only my father can—

NATHAN: *(Slapping her again.)* Ayneleh ...

AYN: *(Very vulnerable, feminine.)* Yes, my darling.

> *(She hugs him.)*

NATHAN: Are you my girl? Are you my beautiful little girl?

AYN: Oh yes, I am. I love you. *(Pause.)* Do you love me?

NATHAN: Yes I do, of course I do. How could you think I wouldn't love you my little bright eyes.

AYN: Bright eyes ... say that again ... I like it better *(She laughs helplessly.)* It sounds so American ...

NATHAN: Bright eyes.

(He kisses her on the eyes.)

AYN: I'm sorry.

NATHAN: Don't be sorry. Get it right. *(He slaps her gently, again.)* Now a minute or two ago, Ayneleh, you had trouble expressing yourself.

AYN: Yes, I did.

NATHAN: You, who has such a way with words.

AYN: *(Ashamed.)* I know.

NATHAN: So now, I want you to tell me what it is that a man does to a woman.

AYN: I can't.

NATHAN: *(Grabbing her, holding her.)* Yes you can—

AYN: No—I can't—

NATHAN: Say it, what you want from me.

AYN: Please—

(He shakes her.)

NATHAN: Ayneleh. Can you say the word, inside?

AYN: Inside?

NATHAN: There we go. That wasn't so bad, was it?

AYN: No.

NATHAN: Now we're going to use that word in a sentence. Say "I want you inside me."

AYN: I want you … inside me.

NATHAN: There.

(He slaps her, lightly. She screams a little, and pants lightly with desire.)

There. Now listen to me. This is what I want to say to you. You're quite right that I'm a little bit uncomfortable today, and you're quite right that though I was completely ready, I made a man's decision. A decision not to do what you just asked me. And do you know why?

AYN: No.

NATHAN: For one simple reason. Because my wife and your husband are out taking a walk and they will be back any minute, and—

AYN: But—

NATHAN: Listen to me.

AYN: Yes sir.

NATHAN: And we have told them, we have in fact promised them that we will not be intimate in that way that a man and woman are especially intimate … how can I act like a man with you under these circumstances? If I do that then we will have let ourselves go. And then we will be lying.

AYN: *(Beginning to become herself again—an intellectual discovery.)* Of course my darling, of course you are right. It is an error of cognition on my part. Of course of course. We must tell them the truth.

NATHAN: *(Concerned, taking a cigarette.)* Well, I don't know *Ayn*. I don't know if we should tell them. Do you think they can handle it?

AYN: But *Nathan*, you give me no choice. We cannot consummate our love unless we tell them. We must tell them that we are planning a love affair. Then we will both be relaxed and free to love each other.

NATHAN: But how will they react to that? You saw how they reacted today.

AYN: They are rational people.

NATHAN: Look at the facts.

AYN: Look at reason.

NATHAN: I don't know if we will ever convince them.

AYN: Don't you see. It does not matter if they are convinced. We are right. They must agree.

NATHAN: But—

AYN: My resolve is renewed. This always happens when I spend time alone with you my darling.

NATHAN: If we're going to tell them soon, then will you do me a favour?

AYN: Of course darling, anything.

NATHAN: Don't tell Frank about the school.

AYN: You mean about—

NATHAN: About my idea to set up a school to teach your principles of Objectivism.

AYN: But Nathaniel, I've told you again and again, I hate the idea of a school—

NATHAN: Oh—Ayn—*(He kisses her.)* I'm not going to talk with you about the details now. You know what will happen if I do. I will insist that if we do not found a learning institution, to spread your ideas, then we are underestimating your philosophy, and your brilliance. I will tell you again that you owe it to the world—

AYN: I don't owe anybody anything.

NATHAN: You owe it to yourself and to a man of supreme intelligence who values you. You owe it to me.

AYN: *(Flustered.)* So you don't want me to—what—

NATHAN: I'm asking you not to discuss the idea of the Objectivist school with Frank until he has become accustomed to our ... relationship.

AYN: Well of course I won't. Why would I? I don't even want this stupid school that you're talking about, I—

NATHAN: Shh ... Ayneleh ... you talk too much.

AYN: I love it when you call me that ... You can do anything you know ... anything you want to stop me from talking ...

> *(He kisses her. He climbs on top of her on the couch as if to make love to her. Lights dim to black. Up on BARBARA and FRANK who are walking beside a bench near a doorway. It is now night.)*

BARBARA: *(Stopping at the door.)* Well here we are.

FRANK: Yes.

BARBARA: I didn't think we'd be walking this way.

FRANK: What do you mean?

BARBARA: I mean ... maybe I should just go inside.

FRANK: We said that we would go back to the apartment.

BARBARA: I know we did.

FRANK: I thought you didn't want to go home.

BARBARA: I didn't want to go home *with him*.

FRANK: Why not? *(He stares at her.)* Why don't we sit down.

BARBARA: *(As they do.)* All right. Because he'll want to psychoanalyze me.

FRANK: You don't like that?

BARBARA: Sometimes I don't, no. *(Pause.)* We've walked a long time. *(Pause.)* I'm cold.

FRANK: Here—have my scarf.

BARBARA: No, I—

FRANK: I'm not cold at all. In fact it's warm.

(He takes it off and gives it to her and she puts it on.)

BARBARA: Thank you. I'm sorry I'm cold.

(Pause. They sit for a moment.)

I know when it happened.

FRANK: When what happened.

BARBARA: When they—ughgh—*(She makes a face.)* connected.

FRANK: When?

BARBARA: When we were driving back from Toronto. You know—after my sister's wedding—

FRANK: Yes, yes—

BARBARA: I saw them looking at each other. In the car.

FRANK: In the car?

BARBARA: Yes. Looking at each other ... the way people look at each other, when—I mean I know that he's always adored her, in his way, but I never thought—

FRANK: I never, never thought.

BARBARA: You didn't?

FRANK: No.

BARBARA: It was evident to me.

(Pause.)

FRANK: Well, remember I was driving.

BARBARA: Oh yes, you were. *(Pause.)* I mean, if I am truly rational about this as well—

FRANK: And you must be.

BARBARA: Nathan and I have been having some problems.

FRANK: We know that, yes.

BARBARA: I've had a hard time, relaxing with him, as a wife.

FRANK: Yes, I know. Ayn told me.

BARBARA: So, I mean, it's not as if we're not having problems ... I know I have to check my premises ... because my ... emotions don't always match my values ...

(She trails off. Pause. They both stare ahead.)

Have you and Ayn been having any problems?

FRANK: No. *(Pause.)* For all of our twenty-six years of marriage we have never had any of ... what you call ... problems.

BARBARA: Twenty-six years. That's such a long time.

FRANK: Yes, it is.

BARBARA: You must love her very much.

FRANK: Yes, I do.

BARBARA: I mean I love Nathan too, he is my highest value, but sometimes he can just be so exasperating.

FRANK: Ayn is always exasperating, but that's another reason why I love her. *(He turns to her.)* Listen to me, Barbara. You know that Ayn is always right.

BARBARA: Is she?

FRANK: I thought you would know that by now.

BARBARA: I know that she's a brilliant woman but—

FRANK: Are you doubting her?

BARBARA: No, of course not, but—

FRANK: She's a genius. She's that very rare thing. A person who sees the truth clearly. She has never allowed her reason to be clouded by emotion. She always ruthlessly checks her premises. In this case though, I wonder about something. You understand that if I love Ayn so dearly that I want only what is best for her, don't you?

BARBARA: Even if that means that she loves another man?

FRANK: Yes even … even that. Can I ask you something about Nathaniel?

BARBARA: Of course.

FRANK: How … ambitious is he?

BARBARA: What do you mean?

FRANK: I know that ambition is a value. I'm wondering how high a value it is for him.

BARBARA: Well … he chases after goals. He's working hard to get his therapy degree. He's goal-oriented. If that's what you mean. We all are.

FRANK: That's not exactly what I mean. I guess I'm asking you … do you think he's really, truly in love with Ayn.

BARBARA: I don't think I'd want to know that if it was true. There's such a big difference between love and *in* love. Now if they just loved each other, I would understand that but you said that they were … I can't even say it … how can you stand to think about that?

FRANK: I can stand it. It all has to do with value. If you think about it rationally.

BARBARA: I know, I know … but, well, all he ever does is talk about her! Which is … understandable of course. She's the centre of our lives. Of all our lives.

FRANK: Of course.

BARBARA: Why would you ask me about his feelings for her?

FRANK: I want to make sure she's doing the right thing.

BARBARA: But Frank really. Be honest—as a man—I mean it's one thing for a woman to have to endure this thing.

FRANK: *(Staunchly.)* I am a man of reason.

BARBARA: Would you be a man of reason if you thought they were … being intimate right now?

FRANK: But they're not.

BARBARA: They *told* us they're not.

FRANK: I could never think that about Ayn. Didn't you see how ruthlessly honest and fair she was? Even today telling us that?

(Pause. BARBARA wilts under all this reason.)

BARBARA: Frank … would you mind holding me? I'm awfully cold …

FRANK: Sure. It's not cold though.

BARBARA: I know … that's what I'm afraid of … you see sometimes, when I get cold it's because … well I don't know if Nathan has ever told you but I do get this anxiety problem now and then—

FRANK: Ayn mentioned something about it, I think—

BARBARA: I just get very anxious, and it's like this cloud this dark cloud—

FRANK: A dark cloud of unreason—

BARBARA: Of unreason, yes and the thing that I'm afraid of is that this cold feeling is just … is just that horrible anxiety coming on, I hope … I hope this whole incident hasn't triggered my anxiety …

FRANK: Use your mind, Barbara. Your reasoning is your protection against unreason.

(Pause.)

BARBARA: I know you're right, of course you're right.

FRANK: I'm right. And Ayn's right too.

BARBARA: I know that. I know that in my head. *(She cuddles up to him.)* But I'm … I'm cold …

(She shivers. He holds her. Blackout.

Lights up on the cliff. MARCEL stands near the edge, alone for a moment.)

MARCEL: Bruce? What are you doing? I really want you to see this view.

BRUCE: *(Still eying him warily.)* I'm putting away all the stuff.

MARCEL: You don't have to do that now. Look, look at how beautiful it is. *(He looks at BRUCE and realizes he must reassure him.)* There's something about being up so high. You can see things you never saw before. Everything becomes perfectly clear.

(He puts his hand on BRUCE's hand, stopping him from clearing up, gently, seductively.)

And then you know exactly … exactly what you have to do. *(He sits down, looking over the edge.)* There you can see the turnpike there … and all the way out into Pennsylvania. Lots of woods in Pennsylvania. Woods and hunters. I went through there on the bus once. There was nothing but woods and hunters and places for people to buy guns.

BRUCE: That sounds awful.

(He sits down and puts his arm around MARCEL.)

What are you thinking, Marcel?

MARCEL: Nothing much. About Pennsylvania and hunters.

(He lies back on the grass, seductively.)

BRUCE: *(Gazing down at him lustfully.)* You know Marcel, I like the way you've grown up.

MARCEL: You do?

BRUCE: Yes. I do.

MARCEL: That's nice.

BRUCE: You've grown up from a delicate boy to a big strong man.

MARCEL: I guess I have.

BRUCE: I like you.

MARCEL: You do?

BRUCE: I like you alot.

MARCEL: I see.

(Pause. MARCEL sits up. BRUCE starts to feel his bum.)

Please don't put your hand there.

BRUCE: What?

MARCEL: I said, please don't put your hand there.

BRUCE: *(Thinking he's playing hard to get.)* But—

MARCEL: Get away from me!

> *(He pushes BRUCE who is about to fall over the cliff, but grabs the tree.)*

BRUCE: Ahhh—Marc—help me—oh my God ... help me ...

> *(He is holding onto the tree with this legs dangling over the edge.)*

MARCEL: *(Suddenly raging.)* I see, you call upon your *God.* Now is the time you call upon your ineffectual *God* to help you. *But there is no God!! (He shouts at him.)* Do you hear me? *God is dead you second-hander—you're nothing but a second-hander like Peter Keating that's what you are Peter Keating Peter Keating Peter Keating—*

BRUCE: *(Struggling.)* Please, *Marc* help me—please—

MARCEL: Are you sorry? Are you sorry now because let me tell you Mr. Molester it wasn't fun for me. You molested me. We didn't diddle together or whatever you call it. You were a man and and I was a boy and I was your victim and *I am not a homosexual* even though you tried to make me into one—

BRUCE: I'm sorry, I tell you I'm sorry—

MARCEL: I don't believe you, and I am a rational person. Besides I don't know what good it will do for you to apologize, because you're an evil person, *evil do you hear me. And you must be punished.* I think I should kick your hands that's what I think I should do. I should kick the hands of the man who molested a poor innocent boy because let me tell you—

BRUCE: No, please no—help me—

MARCEL: *Because (He pulls out his copy of* The Fountainhead.*)* Because there is no negotiating with evil there is no compromise and I went to *Ayn Rand* and I asked her and she said you deserved to die and you do because you're evil and *evil* doesn't deserve to live—

BRUCE: *Please help me—*

MARCEL: I'm not going to help you. I'm going to kick your hands—

BRUCE: *No please no please don't no—*

> *(He kicks his hand.)*

Ahhhh!!

> *(BRUCE's one hand is waving, he's trying to hold on with the other.)*

MARCEL: There, you evil second-hander, you molester—

BRUCE: *(Crying.)* Please help me, please I'm sorry dear God I'm sorry please help me—

MARCEL: No. I'm not going to help you. You're evil and you don't deserve to live, I think I'm just going to kick your other hand—

BRUCE: No please no please no please no—

MARCEL: I'm living up to my highest value. There is no compromise with evil! There!

> *(He kicks him. BRUCE screams and falls out of sight to his death. The lights dim as MARCEL eats another Fig Newton.*
>
> *The lights come up on Ayn and Frank's apartment. All the lights are out except for one by the window; it is very dark. AYN sits there by herself, lit by moonlight. We can see the smoke from her cigarette. Then the door opens a crack, and light falls through, as at the beginning of the play. The door closes. We see FRANK's silhouette. He stands by the door, inside the room, listening, watching, waiting. Pause.)*

AYN: Frank.

FRANK: Ayn.

AYN: Where were you, my darling?

FRANK: Barbara began to get very frightened. I took her home.

AYN: I worry about her.

FRANK: We all do.

> *(Pause. They are still for a moment.)*

How was your discussion with Nathan?

> *(Pause. AYN says nothing for a moment.)*

AYN: *(Warmly.)* Frank, please sit down.

FRANK: All right.

> *(He sits down. AYN puts on a light. They stare at each other, in opposite chairs. But it is still difficult to make out their faces in the semi-dark.)*

AYN: *(Genuinely.)* How are you, Frank?

FRANK: *(A little smile.)* I'm all right.

AYN: Good. *(Pause; not melodramatically.)* You know that you will always be my first and only true love.

> *(Pause.)*

FRANK: *(Smiling.)* Yes, I know that.

AYN: Frank, I want to talk to you about something.

FRANK: Yes.

AYN: Nathan and I talked very deeply this afternoon, it was a very important afternoon, and we came to some conclusions. These conclusions, of course we want to discuss openly, with you and Barbara. But I've decided to talk to you, well, first because, after today, I've certainly seen that Barbara can be well, volatile.

FRANK: She is what I think you and Nathaniel would call, an emotionalist.

AYN: Yes, I'm afraid there is little hope for those like her, who use emotions as tools of cognition.

FRANK: Unlike us.

AYN: Unlike you and I and … and Nathan.

FRANK: And Nathan. And what did you want to tell me, Ayn. Does it involve you and Nathan?

AYN: Yes Frank.

FRANK: I'm ready.

> *(They look at each other warmly, trustingly.)*

AYN: I knew you would be. That's why I love you. *(Pause.)* Frank, I— you must understand that what I am asking of you is something that I would not ask of any other man. It's because of my enormous respect for you and for the powers of your mind that I can speak to you more frankly than I could ever speak to anyone else. You are my equal. Nathan is my intellectual equal. He matches me argument for argument. *You* are my emotional equal. You are much stronger than I. And yet you can see the world with a piercing clarity that matches my own perceptions, though I am the greatest epistemologist the world has ever known. *(Pause. She leans forward.)* Frank, we are special people. We are very special. We are not like the others. Because we are so special, we must live special lives. I think of that horrible little man who came to see me today, that inconsequential Mr. … what—

FRANK: Pin.

AYN: Yes, Pin. The world is filled with people like that. People who misinterpret me. People who strangle all the sense out of my work. They are so limited and so inferior. Sometimes I think that only the finest minds, the special ones, are ready for my philosophy, are ready to live in the world I have created. And we are two of those special people. And this is the beginning of our very special life together. Are you ready?

(Pause.)

FRANK: Yes.

AYN: Nathan and I talked. We talked continuously from the moment that you left with Barbara until moments before you returned. We pored over the situation in agonizing detail. We discussed things which … I have never discussed before and which I never wish to discuss again.

(They both laugh, warmly.)

And we have come to one conclusion. The honest thing which we must do is—Nathan and I we must … be intimate with each other.

(Pause. She sits back and waits. He says nothing. But it would be evident to anyone, except for AYN, that it is as if he has been shot with a gun in the gut.)

Well? *(Pause.)* What is your response?

FRANK: *(Very quietly.)* I have no response.

AYN: How can you have no response.

FRANK: I just … don't.

(Pause.)

AYN: If you disagree with our conclusions Frank, you must say so.

FRANK: I have nothing to say.

AYN: Frank please. You always argue with me. You always match me point for point. I cannot believe that there is nothing that you have to say to me.

FRANK: There is nothing.

(Pause.)

AYN: But you must.

(Pause. She stands up and walks away from him, with her back to him. She considers for a moment, then comes to his conclusion for him. She laughs, lightly.)

Then I take it that you do not object. *(Pause.)* I take it that your lack of argument is a tacit agreement?

(Pause.)

FRANK: You may … take it *(Carefully.)* as anything you wish.

(He is controlling himself with terrible intensity now. But she doesn't notice.)

AYN: *(Happily.)* Then I will. *(Pause.)* Frank, I knew you would understand.

(Pause.)

FRANK: Did you?

AYN: I always knew that you were a very special man.

> *(Pause. They sit in silence for a moment. She plays a few notes on the piano, then closes the piano lid.)*

I am terribly tired. I feel like Atlas. I feel that the weight of the whole world is on my shoulders.

FRANK: It is.

AYN: I don't think I can possibly smoke another cigarette. You know … I would smoke in my sleep if I could. I would smoke and drink coffee and argue in my sleep.

FRANK: Sometimes you do.

AYN: Do I?

FRANK: Yes. You argue with yourself, all the time.

AYN: When I'm sleeping?

> *(FRANK nods.)*

You've never told me that before.

FRANK: There are many things that I have never told you.

AYN: You constantly surprise me. And you always will. My beloved. My very first true love. *(She turns off another light, so that only a light near the window remains.)* Are you coming?

FRANK: I will follow.

AYN: All right. Good night, my beloved.

FRANK: Good night.

> *(She goes out the door to the hallway. FRANK sits in the chair alone for a moment. Then suddenly, he throws his head back and lets out an incredible moan. He clutches the arms of the chair. And then he begins to cry. It comes from very deep inside him. All of the pain, all of the hurt, from the point at which he gave up his sense of his own self for her, comes out. He cries for his bondage to her, and for the end of his emotional life. The music is the fourth "Fantasie-Tableaux" by Rachmaninoff. He struggles up to turn out the lights. The music stops abruptly when the lights in the room snap to black. Crossfade to the bench beside the doorway. Suddenly MARCEL rushes in. He is very excited, tired, panting. He bangs on the door.)*

MARCEL: Mr. Branden! *Mr. Branden. Mr. Brandennn!!*

> *(The door opens suddenly. NATHANIEL stands there in his pyjamas.)*

NATHAN: Can I help you?

MARCEL: Are you the Objectivist therapist?

NATHAN: Yes, but I'm sorry it's—

MARCEL: Thank you. *(He grabs him, and kisses him quickly and spontaneously.)* Thank you.

NATHAN: Get your hands off me—Shit what are you—

>*(He pushes him away.)*

MARCEL: *(Bouncing around.)* I'm not *musical!!* Do you hear me? I killed off every musical part of me! I'm tone deaf! I can't sing a note!

NATHAN: Excuse me—

>*(He tries to shut the door.)*

MARCEL: *(Barring the door.)* No … I want to tell you—how I got all the music out of me! What it feels like to be rid of all the music!

NATHAN: Go away. Jesus Christ! Are you nuts? Are you totally insane. Fucking Jesus Christ you stupid fucking moron. You asshole—hey Barbara, you should see this fucking guy—

>*(He pushes MARCEL to the ground and shuts the door. Pause.)*

MARCEL: *(Standing at the door, he makes his wrist go limp and laughs.)* No more music … I can't even carry a tune … *La la la la la!*

>*(He shouts with no musical value the name for the musical note.)*

La la la la la la!

>*(Then he turns to the audience fiercely and shouts.)*

La!!

>*(Crossfade to Ayn and Frank's apartment. The door to the hall opens and AYN comes in wearing a very elegant bathrobe. She carefully closes the hall door behind her. She turns on the light beside her chair and goes to the phone. She sits with her back to the hall door. She dials and waits for it to ring.)*

AYN: Oh darling … darling, I just had to talk to you, I was so afraid *she* would answer. You know if *she* answered I would have hung up. *(Pause.)* Yes I told him. *(Pause.)* Like the man of reason he is. *(Pause.)* Like the man I love … like my prototype for the perfect man. *(Pause.)* He betrayed no emotion. He *was* Howard Roark. *(Pause.)* You see, for him emotions have never been tools of cognition. He loves me and I love him and I love you, and I think in his own way he loves you too. *(Pause.)* Oh yes.

(She laughs, helplessly again. The door to the hallway opens. The gigantic shadow of a man—FRANK—falls over her. She does not notice. She continues on passionately.)

You may do whatever you wish with me! Whatever you wish! You know that you are the only person I can laugh with now. Do you know that? I dare not show anyone else this laugh. Because it is a truly rational laugh. Listen to it. *(Pause. She laughs.)* Yes. It's like music! Like … Rachmaninoff! It is a deserved laugh. The laugh of a woman at the height of her rational love for her perfect man. Listen darling. Listen …

(She laughs again.

Lights up on MARCEL standing, on the edge of the cliff, his shirt off, his red hair shining in the moonlight.)

MARCEL: Howard Roark laughed.

(He laughs. AYN laughs, still on the phone. The laughter mixes with Rachmaninoff's music—an "Etude-Tableaux." The lights dim on AYN and MARCEL laughing, and FRANK listening. We hear the beginning of the fourth "Fantasie-Tableaux" by Rachmaninoff as the lights hit black. The end.)